ABE MARTIN'S
BARBED WIRE

ABE MARTIN
of Brown County, Indiana

ABE MARTIN'S BARBED WIRE

By

KIN HUBBARD

Author of HOSS SENSE AND NONSENSE

INDIANAPOLIS

THE BOBBS-MERRILL COMPANY

PUBLISHERS

To

THE FARMER

WHO SEEMS TO BE UP AGAINST ABOUT

EVERYTHING BUT THE GOUT

ABE MARTIN'S
BARBED WIRE

Abe Martin's Barbed Wire

BUSINESS CONDITIONS

BY

YILE HURST

YILE HURST, finance an' traffic editur o'
th' Weekly Slip Horn, contributes a highly illuminatin' article on business conditions. His conclusions are given t' th'
public after a brain rackin' survey, an' are
refreshin'ly frank an' clear, with no effort
made t' magnify or minimize conditions as
he found 'em. Ther's nothin' alarmin'
about his report. Rather we find much
that is encouragin' t' th' wage earner an'
investor alike, an' undoubtedly th' general
trend is toward better times, nothin' big,

perhaps, but a general loosenin' up. Some discouragin' situations have been dragged int' th' open, but we must not allow 'em t' blind us t' much that is good an' promisin'. Transient business at th' New Palace hotel is th' worst since 1874, but th' tricounty Shrine gatherin' fer th' first week o' June is expected t' balance things up, an' carry th' hotel over till fall, when th' beds are expected t' fill up agin. Th' undertakin' business is twice as good as it ever wuz. Th' blacksmith shop hain't doin' anything, but th' sody fountain an' magazine department, added in December, more'n pay th' overhead. Th' Emporium is doin' some little dry goods business, an th' glassware department reports sherbert glasses movin' satisfactorily. Draperies an' petticoats are sluggish, but th' hot dog steam table an' slot phone had th' best June in seven years. Th' tile works took a little spurt Monday, but closed down Friday

till next Thursday. March marked th'
first time spats wuz ever sold here, th'
sales exhaustin' th' supply. Silk hose show

Mr. Yile Hurst

no let down, an' keepin' supplied has been
th' principal concern of our merchants.
Th' demand fer cocktail shakers contin-

13

ues. However, th' sale o' these contraptions is so widely distributed that no single merchant seems t' have th' edge, unless it would be Bentley's harness store. Also Joe Means, th' florist, sells a heap o' them. They're a profitable side line fer any business. Mrs. Joe Spry, our leadin' hemstitcher, sold eighteen in August. Th' O. K. livery barn is open, an' that's about all. This is attributed t' th' auto, which is here t' stay. Our auto business out-distanced all other years. Pianner business is indifferent, an' way below former years, owin', no doubt, t' th' general an' widespread collapse o' th' home as a place o' entertainment. Ther's been an' alarmin' fallin' off o' after supper business downtown, candy stores an' picture houses sufferin' thereby. This situation kin, o' course, be traced directly t' th' radio, a comparatively new diversion, which is expected t' gradually wear down t' somethin' borderin' on san-

14

ity. Diamonds an' pearls are at a stand-still owin' t' costume jewelry bein' all th' rage. Skirt plays have starved t' death at Melodeon Hall, but "musical" shows have pulled down considerable money. Our library announces a most gratifyin' demand fer darin'ly frank fiction, an' a new pool table wuz unveiled at th' Smoke House th' first o' th' month.

Why does a prescription allus cost around seventy-five cents regardless o' what's in it?

Another traffic nuisance is th' feller who pokes along eight miles an hour while tryin' t' cop a girl off th' curb.

15

Some fellers drink so they'll be pleasant, an' some women paint so they kin wear gray.

Th' race would die out if it wuzn' fer children, an' besides they give a wife somethin' t' live fer.

Th' new thirty-three-inch silk stockin's ought t' enable 'em t' step in a rumble seat without gittin' sunburned.

"He hain't got no education, an' he's triflin' an' won't look fer work, an' he won't even write a pop'lar song so his paw won't have t' support him," said Mrs. Lile Lark, speakin' of her son.

16

Some folks attend t' ther own business, an' others stop along th' sidewalks an' confuse those who'er tryin' t' back out of a parkin' place.

Ther's plenty o' peace in any home where th' family don't make th' mistake o' tryin' t' git t'gether.

Th' first thing a feller does when he's held up is change his mind about what he used t' think he'd do.

At a debate at Apple Grove Schoolhouse, it wuz resolved that th' fishin' worm is a better friend o' th' farmer than Sen. Capper.

SOCIETY AN' PERSONAL

BY

MISS WANDA KITE

ONE o' th' social surprises o' th' wanin' summer wuz th' purty weddin' o' Miss Babe Kite an' Mr. Buck Tanger, solemnized at high noon Thursday in th' basement o' th' Court House, an' th' happy culmination of a romance that begun durin' a dry raid at th' Purple Turtle barbecue.

_____

Albert Moots, fifteen, th' interestin' son o' Mr. and Mrs. Tilford Moots, long prominent in uplift circles, wuz th' only boy in a class o' fourteen that wuzn' detained fer further examination in th' investigation o' th' Monarch 5 & 10 burglary.

18

Mr. Lionel Moots, a pop'lar member o' th' local younger set, reports that he got as fer as Frederick, Maryland, in a stolen Ford before he wuz arrested, thereby winnin' first prize in th' "Stolen Ford Run" on th' National Road between Greenfield, Indianny, an Washin'ton.

———

Alec Craw, prominent an' well t' do farmer, has been missin' ever since steps wuz taken t' analyze his wife's stomach, an' foul play is feared.

———

A joyous throng filled th' beautiful home o' Pustmaster Lisle Tharp in honor o' th' seventh weddin' anniversary o' th' pop'lar Hoover worker an' his charmin' wife. Many remarked on th' absence o' th' usual murkiness in th' home-made beer, Mrs. Tharp explainin' that she lets it set forty hours instead o' thirty, an' syphons it twice, thereby eliminatin' much sediment.

———

Our readers kin well imagine th' joy that filled th' Laurel Kite home last evenin' when, after weeks o' anxiety, a telegram wuz received from ther daughter, Miss Tiny, fourteen, sayin,' "Don't worry stop I'm in Chicago stop."

———

Mrs. Art Purviance is visitin' her husband an' babies.

———

Mr. Elmer Kale, who'll be recalled as th' husband o' Mrs. Letty Kale, prominent social worker, will address th' Woman's Department Club on th' care o' th' home an' children.

Mrs. Lafe Bud, who wuz recently choked an' robbed by burglars, didn't call th' police as she'd jest had her floors gone over.

———

Mr. an' Mrs. Jake Bentley, th' justly proud parents o' Leonard an' Clifford Bentley, twins an' seventeen, who won first an' second prizes in th' chair-canin' contest at th' Pendleton Reformatory, have placed photergraphs o' th' youngsters in th' north window o' th' Elite Drug & Sandwich Shop.

———

Easily th' classiest an' most successful social affair o' th' early fall wuz th' house warmin' at th' Skunk Ridge Golf an' Country Club's new winter home. No wife tradin'. No arrests. No deaths.

21

PHYSIOGNOMY

BY

Mrs. Pogue Swallow

Professor Hawk, physiognomist, room 8, New Palace Hotel, is here fer a limited stay, an' offers his services t' all who wish t' know what walk in life is best suited t' ther talents. Many who'er already established in life, many who'er thinkin' o' makin' a change, an' others who'er jest flounderin' around, are availin' 'emselves o' th' opportunity t' consult th' Professor. Jest t' show how people kin git off on th' wrong foot we herewith present th' portraits an' readin's o' four prominent citizens.

No. 1. Tilford Moots, retired farmer. Note th' low an' somewhat bulgin' forehead, flopper-like ears, an' sparse chin

22

whiskers. Mr. Moots wuz a farmer fer forty-five years without knowin' he would

Familiar Faces

excel as an oil inspector, or big game hunter. He drifted int' agriculture an' wasted almost a half-century of his life.

No. 2. Miss Mame Moon. Note th' wide open space between th' septum o' th' nose an' th' bottom o' th' chin. Note th' low Moorish forehead an' liberal neck, thin lips, an' wealth o' coarse black hair. This subject has spent th' greater part of her life operatin' a livery stable, an' now in her declinin' years her whole time is taken up tryin' t' git somebuddy t' buy it an' convert it into an apartment buildin'. Th' septum of her nose is not discernible in th' accompanyin' picture, but it's fully developed an' vigorous. Th' subject has not buried four husbands as th' reader might suspect. Matrimony has never occurred t' her. She started out in life utterly ignorant of her talents. She would have been invaluable t' science in diggin' up prehistoric animals, an' peculiarly successful in leadin' expeditions into Tibet an' th' Gobi desert.

No. 3.   Constable Newt Plum. From what we're able t' see o' this gentleman's features he would have gone fer as a hog raiser, but he didn' git his head examined, an' so he drifted.

No. 4.   Hiram Meadows. Note th' long thin parchment nose, his big underslung ears, an' dry ferret's gray, penetratin' eyes, tiny chin an' well rounded Adam's apple. This subject is open an' above board. Ther's nothin' deceptive about him or he'd raise a full beard. He might have been a high an' commandin' figure in any honorable walk in life. He is a fruit tree agent, an' might be said t' live comfortable, although he has no phone an' only one bathroom.

Why are only Democratic candidates ever asked how wet or dry they are?

"Slip me some mad money, maw," said Miss Gert Mopps, an' then her maw explained that that meant some change t' git home on if her daughter's beau got fresh, or too drunk t' drive.

Th' feller that's still carryin' th' same dinner bucket he started out with thirty years ago don't seem t' care fer luncheon clubs an' mass thinkin'.

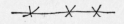

That Texas toad that lived so long buried in rock hain't got nothin' on a Republican I know, who has existed out o' office fer nearly three years.

26

I like Lafe Bud 'cause he's allus so orig-
inal an' different. Lately he said he'd jest
grabbed a job, instead o' sayin' he'd ac-
cepted a position.

I expect th' reason a considerable per
cent o' girls leave home is 'cause ther's
somethin' creepy about stayin' there
alone.

Th' minute it looked like th' McNary-
Haugen bill might pass, Farmer Jake
Bentley called up an' ordered a second car.

Who recalls th' ole-time grocery with
ever'thin' uncovered an' exposed, an' a big
maltese cat asleep in th' prunes?

27

Th' Seattle girl who recently married a former maharajah o' Indore may not know it, but a Hindoo honeymoon only lasts till th' first girl baby.

"Makin' both ends meet is gittin' t' be such a problem that I hain't bought a thing fer th' house 'cept some seat covers fer th' car," says Mrs. Pogue Swallow.

While Indianny politicians usually have their mitts out, they serve a term fer nothin' now an' then.

Ike Soles fell in th' mill pond while lookin' fer a golf ball, but his flask kept him afloat till his cries fer help wuz heard.

Some folks are born in society, an' some are coaxed in, but a large per cent o' them tunnel in.

Ther's no industrial turmoil or factory whistles in Washin'ton, but Jake Bentley's nephew wants t' sell his home there on account o' Senator Heflin.

There seems t' be an excess o' ever'-thing 'cept parkin' space an' religion.

It seems like th' day's gone by when really first-class men kin be elected t' office, an' even slippin' one over by appointment hain't allus as easy as it looks.

Th' Emporium announces th' arrival of a new consignment o' size 6 hats fer "100 per cent Americans."

A late census shows that ther's only 69,-501 blacksmiths left, that is, blacksmiths who admit it.

Two-year terms fer gov'nors makes presidential timber of them entirely too soon.

Lisle Tharp, whose father left him two farms, has petitioned t' have th' will set aside, declarin' his father must have been crazy.

"We wuz afraid somethin' might have happened t' him, but we called up th' jail, an' ther he wuz, safe an' sound, so our worry wuz all fer nothin'," said Mrs. Joe Kite, whose boy didn' show up fer breakfast.

I kin remember when I wuz a little boy, cigarettes wuz goin' t' kill Sam Ackison, but I saw him in town this fall lookin' like a million dollars.

"Well, she kin afford a husband fer she's got a good job, an' has allus saved her money," snapped Mrs. Em Pash, when somebuddy knocked Miss Babe Kite's engagement.

31

I don't know why we still call 'em th' weaker sex, unless it's because they allus ask us t' lift th' pianner while they slip a corner of a rug under it.

Th' commonest mistake o' all is thinkin' a hat'll do fer another season.

Mrs. Ike Soles' niece, o' Chicago, writes that her husband had injured his spine actin' as pall bearer fer a slug-filled ward boss.

Jealousy is at th' bottom o' most o' th' criticism o' th' younger generation.

32

A TIMELY DEBATE

BY

ONE WHO WUZ THERE

"WHICH Has Been th' Greatest Factor in
Demoralizin' Our Nation—Jazz Music or
th' Automobile?" wuz debated at Apple
Grove School, No. 8. Miss Emmy Louise
Moots took th' auto side an' Mr. Bib
Tharp took jazz music. Miss Moots led
off as follers: "Ever'thing that's bad an'
ornery, an' sensational an' scandalous, an'
crooked an' contrary t' right livin', that's
goin' on in our fair country t'day kin be
traced directly t' th' automobile. Th' automobile is a wonderful invention an' neces-
sary t' our happiness, an' in th' promotion
o' legitimate business. Th' gasoline tax
makes good highways possible, while th'

33

license money makes other things possible. Our grocer kin deliver head lettuce an' things faster by auto, an' great movin'

Bib Tharp an' Emmy Louise Moots

vans kin move us without breakin' any canned t'maters. Th' auto has taught us t' think faster an' jump quicker. Th' in-

34

dustry employs many thousands o' mechanics an' advertisin' men who might be a charge on th' community if we wuz still usin' buggies, but ther's another side t' th' story. Th' auto makes it possible fer a feller t' hold up a bank at Milroy, Indianny, an' be back in Muncie in an' hour. Th' auto makes it possible fer lots o' college boys t' thumb ther way home ever' week-end, when they ought t' be catchin' up on sleep. Criminals who used t' escape on technicalities, now grab th' first auto they see. Autos wreck family circles an' knock ole people down. Th' auto has discouraged plowin', an' has made it possible fer city people t' steal cherries an' cucumbers an' visit an' annoy ther country cousins ever' week-end. Some boys steal cars so they kin go with th' girls, an' all boys are sullen an' morose an' impossible t' live with unless they have cars. Pedestrians have t' give their whole time an' thought t'

keep from gittin' killed, often fergittin'
what they come downtown fer, an' allus
gittin' ther calves splashed with oily mud.
Th' auto has made it possible fer a girl t'
tell her mother she'd jest been around th'
corner when she'd really been t' Nobles-
ville. In concludin', I wish t' state that th'
auto has been th' downfall o' more girls
than all th' fur coats an' gin put t'gether."
Mr. Bib Tharp said, "Jazz music, I'm told,
originated in a questionable colored resort
in Baltimore. I don't know how true it is,
but it sounds mighty reasonable t' me.
Think of a great, big, powerful nation like
ours bein' gripped by jazz as nothin' else
within th' memory o' man has ever before
gripped it! Nobuddy kin listen t' jazz
music without squirmin', or doin' somethin' undignified. Ther's somethin' about
jazz music that makes us want t' kick up,
or hug or kiss somebuddy. Th' frightful,
discordant sounds are supposed t' be

funny, while th' grimaces an' gyrations o' the musicians, or windjammers, are reckoned t' be highly divertin'. Th' average jazz drummer's idea o' mirth provokin' is entirely different from anything we used t' know. Jazz music has brought all th' stuff out on th' dance hall floor that used t' be pulled in th' dimly-lighted parlor. It has driven modesty off th' boards, an' substituted a brazenness an' abandon that's shockin', an' I'm not quite twenty-one. Gin an' cigarettes are th' camp followers o' jazz an' I believe car takin' is closely allied. Jazz has taken thousan's o' likely young men out o' th' legitimate channels of endeavor an' made fourth-rate musicians out o' them, an' I hope I won't be here when jazz hits th' rocks an' these thousan's are thrown on th' world. Th' only redeemin' thing about jazz is that it has furnished employment durin' our lean years t' countless throngs o' saxophone makers."

"Well, he'll come in mighty handy if she ever gits tired of her husband," said Squire Marsh Swallow, when he heard that Mrs. Lafe Bud's gran'dad had gone crazy.

Jake Bentley is lettin' his whiskers grow till some state springs a favorite daughter, but if he wants 'em t' git good an' long he ought t' let 'em alone till women git too independent t' accept alimony.

"Ther seems t' be ever'thing in th' Republican party but Albinos," said Tell Binkley, when he read that Senator Curtis, o' Kansas, is half Indian.

38

People are no worse'n they ever wuz. They jest used t' couldn' put th' stuff over with a horse an' buggy.

What becomes o' th' Christmus spirit after Christmus?

Our country has made phenomenal strides along some lines, but we mustn' be too boastful, we mustn' fergit that we dumped 957,491,706 gallons o' sauer kraut juice before we found out we could git ten cents a glass fer it.

I'll say this fer Herbert Hoover—he's one o' the best men Woodrow Wilson ever discovered.

O' course we all can't fly, an' we all can't keep our mouths shut, but if we'd only talk half as much, we'd be learnin' somethin' from Lindy.

When a consumer feels like he needs a double garage he goes down in his pocket an' pays fer it, but when a public utility wants t' expand it makes its customers pay th' bill.

Why don't they shoot a little advice into college students each day instead o' hand-in' it t' 'em all in a lump when they graduate?

40

Th' saddest commentary on our courts is that th' banks now refuse t' pay rewards for bandits on th' hoof.

"I used t' pick up an' haul quite a lot o' folks, but I jest wore myself out tellin' 'em how t' open th' car door," says Lem Pusey.

"I've noticed one thing in th' last few months, hotel clerks quietly shift ther watches t' their trousers pockets when you register from Indianny," says Lafe Bud, who travels fer a crayon portrait concern.

I've often wondered how a feller with a single-track mind sidesteps a new idea when he feels it bearin' down on him.

With all his wealth an' world-wide reputation, I notice that Henry Ford still uses printer's ink.

Ther may be some good in ever'buddy, as th' sayin' goes, but life's too short in this fast age t' hang around till it pops out.

Constable Newt Plum says he'll have Sunday's ax murderer in th' jug before sun down, let th' chips fall where they may.

Lester Kite has quit school on account o' poor parkin' facilities.

42

"I'd hate t' live in a city where nobuddy knows your business unless you spend about fifty thousand dollars a year advertisin' it," says Lyle Spry, o' th' Emporium.

"Oh, I have no regrets. My life has been purty full an' happy, 'cept I've allus wanted t' see an oil quiz," said Gran'-maw Moots, ninety-eight, jest before she passed away.

Remember when th' whole family used t' dress around th' baseburner in th' mornin', an' read around it, an' fight around it? It's furnace heat that put th' ole family circle out o' business.

It seems like th' more science does fer th' kitchen th' more new eatin' places open up downtown.

I used t' think women wuz resourceful, but so fer not a husband has been murdered with a door-stop, an' ther hain't nothin' handier t' hold.

Th' only absolutely safe an' reliable forecast fer 1929 is more deaths, higher taxes, an' a bumper crop o' rhubarb.

France is jest like some people—pleasant an' lovely t' meet, but she won't pay nothin'.

44

HAND-MADE LETTERS

BY

LESTER LARK

ONE o' the finest feelin's ther is t'day comes with gittin' a long, newsy, hand-written letter from an' ole friend. Even an' ole-fashioned, pencil-scribbled Manila pustal card, announcin' th' arrival of a new baby, or th' marriage of a distant cousin causes a thrill. Telegrams, picture cards, an' marked newspapers, an' formal typewritten letters, don't fill th' bill like a good, liberal, amateurish, mussy, hand-made, unpunctuated letter from some-buddy we like. It takes lots o' trouble t' sit down an' turn out a hand-made letter. Ther's considerable labor, an' thought, an' friendship behind a handwrote letter.

Such a letter has somethin' warm an' personal about it that one can't put in a machine-made letter, or on a highly colored picture pustal showin' one hour's catch at Silver Lake. I reckon ther hain't over six or seven regular what I'd call warm ole time letters in a whole truck load o' modern mail. "Have you heard from Ellie?" somebuddy'll ask somebuddy whose Ellie has been gone fer four months. "Yes, we got a picture card from her yisterday mailed at Salt Lake, but we expect her home this week mebbe." I thought th' World War would revive letter writin', an' it did fer awhile, but it soon went th' way o' ever'thing else good that we hoped t' git out o' th' mess. Ther's somethin' hard an' artificial an' forced about a typewritten letter, an' after one uses a typewriter awhile he gits so he can't sign his name so you kin read it. Typewritten letters seem so mechanical an' impersonal, an' I keep

thinkin' it's an' ad, or a touch, an' I'm almost afraid t' read t' th' end. "Do you ever
hear from your son Henry since he got

In Close Touch by Mail

married?" "Oh, yes indeed, we got a telegram only three months ago sayin' he wuz
still married an' wuz jest about t' take his

47

first airplane ride. Ther's been nothin' in the newspapers about him so we reckon he's all right." An' a letter never seems personal that's been dictated t' a frouzy stenographer an' bearin' an' indentifyin' cypher like we find on th' underside of a sweat band. Soldiers that were never known t' write a reg'lar letter in ther lives contributed th' most interestin' literature o' th' World War, letters written in ther own breezy careless fashion with no dictionary within forty thousand kilometers. It does take lots o' work an' trouble t' git squared away t' write a letter by hand, t' git ever'thing t'gether, t' find a blotter an' thin th' ink up, but a real self-executed letter is th' most unique an' acceptable gift you kin send a friend.

"I hain't complainin' about him not bein' a good provider, Judge, but he acts like a perfect brute if I make th' least suggestion about his cookin'," testified Mrs. Leslie Hanger, in divorce court t'-day.

What gits me is how a feller who goes t' Detroit on business keeps in shape t' transact any business.

"Well, if he hadn' escaped in an auto, he'd got out on a habus corpus," said Constable Plum, after a bandit had slipped thro' his fingers.

49

One would think we belonged t' th' league o' nations from th' way "our boys" are bein' mowed down in Nicaraugy.

"It wuz so blamed cold Sunday we jest stayed t' home an' played cards t' see who'd git th' divorce," I heard Mrs. Em Moots remark.

Don't believe ever'thing you read about prosperity. You'll feel it in your pockets when it gits here.

They say Ike Lark's son drinks like a chaperon.

"Well, th' chemist wuz late an' ever'-buddy wuz in an ugly humor, an' I wuz glad when it wuz over," said Lafe Bud, in commentin' on th' Tilford Moots birthday dinner.

After livin' in Herrin, Illinoy, a year, an' bein' a bank cashier three years, an' bein' married two years, Mrs. Tipton Bud's nephew wuz finally run down an' killed by a dray.

Th' big objection t' Hoover fer President is he hain't got no magnetism. That feller Coolidge has set some pace.

51

We can't mix politics with nothin' but office gittin'.

I'll bet Dame Fashion is a brazen ole geezer.

What's worsen' tryin' t' read a news-paper in a buss or street-car full o' yellow knees.

What little courtesy ther is left seems t' be confined entirely t' pedestrians.

Lots o' folks are too proud t' beg, but they seem t' enjoy bein' dunned.

After many years o' th' closest observation I'm more convinced than ever that th' louder a feller laughs at nothin' th' more pop'lar he is.

Next t' bein' mistaken fer a wealthy widder, th' most dangerous thing is lookin' like a deer.

Don't git fooled on purrin'. A cat would attack us in a second if it wuzn' afraid.

Doctor Mopps has allus been in such great demand that he's never seen but one whole play, an' that's "Abie's Irish Rose." He commenced goin' t' see it in 1918, but never saw th' last act till 1928.

Colonel Lindbergh has got it all over other celebrities. He kin excuse himself t' work on his engine.

Sheriff Wes Peters has had t' put th' jail bars closer t'gether t' hold th' kid bandits.

"We are all crazy when we do a lot o' things," said Judge Pusey, in orderin' an alienist out o' th' court-room t'day.

It's said that over eighty per cent o' federal prisoners are educated, which goes t' prove that idleness soon gits us into trouble.

GRAY HAIR, ETC.

BY

CLEM HARNER

THERE is more worryin' over gray hair t'-
day than there is over all other real or im-
aginary troubles combined. Fer many
years attempt after attempt has been
made t' dye gray mustaches a soft natural
black, but th' most heroic efforts have
failed t' produce anything betterin' a
dusty buzzard black. Perhaps th' best results have been obtained by usin' shoe
blackin', but th' steam from th' nose soon
fades out th' center section, givin' th' job
an unfinished appearance. Gun metal mustaches are easily produced by usin' emery
dust an' light oil, but they are easily de-
tected as fer as three blocks on a clear
day, an' are decidedly unnatural lookin'

under electric lights, rarely foolin' th' most unobservin'. But th' great consumption o' hair dyes t'day is amongst th' women, an' ther's no more pathetic sight than a seventy-two-year-ole woman with her hair dyed a battery-cell black. Women should know that gray hair is not a sign of advanced age. Many men an' women are gray before ther twenty-five. Gray hair is hereditary. Neither piety or th' stress o' modern life bothers hair. Ther's few things as strikin' as a purty face set in gray hair, an' few things as awful as an ole mug crowned with dyed hair. People used t' powder ther hair t' make it gray, an' who'd trust a banker that wuzn' gray around th' temples? Women are successful enough in hidin' ther real dispositions, but they've never yit fooled anybuddy by dyin' ther hair. Jest as a gun metal mustache emphasizes a red nose, so does imitation raven hair emphasize an' ole face. Ther's so much personal camaflougin' 'mongst men an' women these days, so many veneered wrecks floatin' about, so many recondi-

Reconditioned Veterans

tioned belles an' beaus on th' market that it's no wonder middle-aged weddin's are only rude awakenin's.

We can't be a gentleman these days without folks edgin' away from us.

Marriage is purty much of a lottery, 'cept we know what sort o' knees we're gittin'.

Doctors say insane people are fer happier than sane people, so I guess lots of our optimists are really optimists after all.

While failure in private business may not be a recommendation fer a political office, it's nearly allus th' real incentive.

Constable Newt Plum's son-in-law up t' Indynoplus, is out o' jail, but still a Republican.

Ther's nothin' in th' newspapers about what Frank W. Stearns chooses t' do about 1928, but it's more'n likely he'll leave th' White House with th' President.

"Well, sir, it wuz th' best I could do at that time," said ole Dan Moss, when asked how in th' world he ever happened t' marry his uncle's widder.

Laugh an' you make wrinkles, weep an' your cheeks run.

59

Bandit Stew Nugent got his knees riddled with buckshot tryin' t' escape in woman's clothes.

"I wouldn' want t' live in a little town where ever'buddy knows ever'buddy else's business," is a common expression, but a pop'lar bank cashier of Arcadia, Ohio, cleaned up $250,000 in lessn' two years without anybuddy gittin' on.

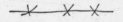

Why call it face liftin', when th' face is stretched much th' same as th' heel of a sock over a darnin' ball an' then anchored back o' th' ears?

"You mark my word, they'll be here when we're dead an' gone," says Gran'-maw Bentley, while deplorin' th' widespread criticism of boys an' girls.

Mrs. Ike Lark is all worked up fer fear her boy'll be drafted fer Thompson's war with England.

I'd never want t' go back t' tallow candles, whiskers, petticoats, an' mud roads, but we certainly could use a few ole-time political leaders if we had 'em t'-day.

I don't believe anybuddy ever used a hammer without swearin'.

61

"Give me a color card," said Miss Fawn Lippincut, when th' doctor told her she'd have t' have her tonsils painted.

Miss Tawney Apple has contracted neuritis from chilled cocktail shakers.

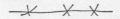

"Her ears are showin' an' she wears shell-rimmed glasses, so I'm not worried about her at all," says Mrs. Em Moots, whose daughter went after a sack o' corn meal over two weeks ago an' has never been heard of since.

A feller will stop at any kind of a hotel if his feet hurt.

Fish-hooks are legal tender 'mongst th' Eskimos, an' a politician tells me that when he's not quite sure of his man he invariably uses a quart instead of money.

Next t' settlin' back an' lightin' a nickel cigar at th' dinner-table, th' worst breach o' good taste is tryin' t' separate a fish-bone from a mouthful o' mashed perta-ters.

Even if he is quiet I'll bet President Coolidge has got a mind of his own an' kin assert himself as well as anybuddy when somethin' goes wrong, fer instance, when th' White House cook bakes too many per-taters.

Next t' an eastbound tramp ther's few things as busy as an Indianny grand jury.

The feller who tries t' be right these days has an awful time gittin' ahead.

A pedestrian stood up fer his rights almost five minutes in Bloom Center.

Who recalls when "darin'ly frank" books had t' be read in a haymow?

CLOTHES AN' PROFESSIONS

BY

TELL BINKLEY

THIRTY years ago most anybuddy would have bet Dudley Purviance wuz a faro dealer instead o' th' president o' th' People's Bank with his bright purple plaid suit o' clothes, white Fedora, an' a big yeller diamond pin. Folks can't tell these days what a feller is up to by th' style of his clothes. Ther used t' be jest one mold o' stiff hat an' two styles o' shoes—commonplace an' alligator. A feller may be a stiff colorless undertaker an' still wear gay Russian pebble grain double-stitched sport shoes. Folks no longer think o' ther professions when they buy things t' wear. Ministers used t' dress like they wuz laid out fer burial. T'day we can't tell a minister from an insurance solicitor. It used t' be possible t' single out doctors an' lawyers by ther shinin' plug hats, but grocers an' nursery salesmen got t' wearin' 'em, an' th' plug hat died out. Th' graceful dressy Prince Albert had a hard struggle. It wuz originally designed fer gentlemen who were some pumpkins, but th' fourth raters, illiterates, an' designin' adventurers were quick t' see its possibilities an' it finally went th' way o' th' plug hat. Gamblers an' actors used t' be our flashiest dressers. You can't tell an actor any more by his dress. An' it's impossible t' git next t' a gambler, even by pallor or scarfpin. Ther's nothin' about our bootleggers t' distinguish them from attorneys or anybuddy carryin' a fat brief-case. We can't even tell by those th' bootlegger calls on whether he's peddlin' th' New Testament, or is goin' t' cut out a corn, or shave a corpse, or deliver some nude silk hose. A deaf man couldn' tell a convention o' veterinary surgeons from a bankers' conven-

Clothes Tell Nothing

tion 'cept by th' odor. Ther's still a few odd an' extreme dressers among all classes o' men, but ther's nothin' telltale about ther clothes. Ther liable t' be up t' most any thing, or as harmless as a dust-mop solicitor.

Any woman that's worse'n she's painted is hardly worth savin'.

Alcohol czars an' beer kings are th' shortest lived of all rulers, rarely livin' half as long as a candidate fer th' Mexican presidency.

Keepin' mum about bein' insane till you git all your murderin' done don't count.

Say whatever else you please about Lon Moon, he's got th' best lookin' Bible class in town.

If Colonel Lindbergh's South American trip really shows results I'm in favor o' sendin' him t' Wisconsin.

Th' hand that rocks th' cradle is just as liable t' rock th' country.

"Anything as tame as he is would git my goat. He don't even curse when a coat hanger falls on th' floor," says Mrs. Em Moots, in speakin' o' Kenneth Kite.

69

These are great days fer judges t' show what ther made of.

By th' time a modern weddin'-day rolls around th' bride's father hain't got nothin' left t' give but a daughter.

After anybuddy gits up around a hundred it goes without sayin' he wuz born in a log cabin.

It must be awful t' be rich an' idle, an' have nothin' t' look forward t' but gittin' all lit up agin.

70

I guess really great people have a purty tryin' time, but overrated folks seem t' enjoy it.

Ther's some little conjecturin' about President Coolidge, but I've never heard o' him bein' misquoted.

A mother's first duty is t' her family an' home. After that it's nobuddy's business how she brandishes her knees.

It's too bad we're not all so constituted as t' endure discouragement an' criticism like a reformer.

71

If th' rich don't know no more about rare tapestries an' costly Rembrandts than they do about counterfit Gordon gin bottle caps, I pity 'em.

"I'll be glad when I'm found guilty, an' git a new trial, an' go free, an' have this mess over with," said Mrs. Tilford Moots' niece, whose late husband wuz insured fer eighteen thousand dollars.

One o' th' worst combinations I know of is lots of initiative an' an offensive personality.

72

It would be fun t' know how many automobile owners make $1.25 an hour same as service station mechanics.

What contented people I've seen looked mighty easily pleased.

What gits me is why so many winnin' streaks seem t' stop so abruptly after a feller wins a bride.

There's nothin' as essential as good, cold-nosed bosses, whether it's a p'litical party, a business concern, or a family o' two.

73

I'd like t' see silver dollars come back. They used t' be mighty handy t' slap on th' counter an' wake up a clerk.

"We did have a hammer, but my husband threw it away," said Mrs. Joe Kite, t' a feller who'd come t' fix th' roof.

I never git excited over nothin', fer I remember when Liberty muffins started off with a big hurrah an' a blare o' trumpets, an' where are they t'day?

Who remembers when bandits wore masks because they wuz afraid o' gittin' in trouble?

Elections scatter money an' eight cent cigars, close banks an' demoralize business, but they've never been known t' lower any taxes.

A feller has t' be mighty patient an' easy goin' to make beer twice.

Lots o' fellers pretend t' resent any instructions from th' back seat when they're really relyin' on 'em.

It seems like you kin pull most anything in a swell café 'cept a pipe.

75

Lester Lark is up against it. He's too ole t' git off with a reprimand, an' he hain't got a car of his own.

I expect lots o' car drivers are charged with intoxication when it's only th' engine th' constable smells.

Next t' battleships ther hain't nothin' gits out o' date as quick as bridegrooms.

"Woman's work is never done"—any more.

76

Modern kitchen equipment makes cookin' almost as simple as th' wife that stays at home an' cooks.

A lot o' green horns still look at women.

Waitin' fer a doctor's bill is jest like waitin' t' be sentenced.

Most so-called contentment is due t' general worthlessness.

New York City, with her 5,970,000 population, would be a dandy place t' lose a relative.

77

PEACE

BY

SQUIRE MARSH SWALLOW

THER'S nothin' as scarce an' short lived as peace. Peace is an ole word an' one that is often used by th' unthinkin'. Webster says this about peace: "Rest or tranquillity; calm; freedom from war or disturbance." Who could hope fer any peace in th' face o' that definition? When we analyze things we realize that anything even borderin' on tranquillity in this day an' age is a myth. We may git a breathin' spell now an' then, but tranquillity is another thing. I doubt if anybuddy ever reached that glorious condition o' body an' mind when it could be truthfully said o' him that he wuz even sittin' purty—unless he wuz dead, an' then it would be a mere speculation. We hear o' connubial peace, an' I'll allow that ther are little spasms o'

The Fullest Freedom

joy an' relaxation from care in th' married state, but ther mighty fleetin', an' all put t'gether they'd comprise a mighty stingy per cent o' th' whole, one, five, or even fifty years, o' harnessed existence. Even in apartments with only cigarette ashes t' carry out, with only three rooms t' dust, no prattle o' children t' disturb th' quiet, no drudgery 'cept connectin' th' toaster, ther's no such thing as peace. Either th' husband has jest been fired, or th' wife's hat hain't fit t' wear, or they've been asked t' move, or th' can opener has been carried away in th' garbage, or ther'll be somethin' t' jim th' tranquillity. Business peace! Business would go t' th' dogs without hot competition an' worry. Industrial peace is th' biggest joke. Ther'll never be industrial peace till workers fix ther own wages, an' then ther won't be peace. As long as people have t' work fer a livin' ther won't be no industrial peace. National peace! Imagine national peace with two big snarlin' political parties, middle west fanatics, western reactionaries, eastern wets, salaried reformers, one hundred per cent Americans, an' periodical elections. I've allus thought that a travelin' umbreller mender came nearer reachin' th' peace goal than any other livin' human. He quietly plies his trade, he has no incumbrances, he's not goin' anywhere in particular, he'll sleep any place, he don't have t' shave, he's never solicited, gits no invitations t' June weddin's an' intellectual treats, has no underwear t' fuss about, an' wears no man's collar. I wuz discussin' peace with an umbreller mender a few days ago, an' he remarked, "Brother, when my wife skipped out twenty years ago I thought my troubles wuz over, but yisterday I found two bridges out on th' road t' Bloom Center."

Lots o' girls an' women seem t' confuse th' bloom of youth with a candy apple.

Human life's so cheap that most auto-ists seem t' feel that it's hardly worth while t' slow down when they kill a pedestrian.

Ther's lots o' things about success that hain't generally known, but ther's no se-crets about failures.

Scar-face Al Capone must have had his face lifted.

It takes a mighty smart feller t' succeed with a good education.

Next t' a third marriage I can't think o' nothin' as tame as th' crownin' of a chess king.

Women kin stand twice as much sufferin' as men, an' as thin as they dress they kin sit a circus out, an' often stay fer th' concert.

I often wonder if there's th' same respect fer a gray toupee as ther is fer a bald head?

"I expected t' be home at ten, but we sat around waitin' an' waitin' fer a kick, till I lost all idee o' time," I could hear Mrs. Lafe Bud yell, as I passed her home late one night.

I don't think th' world's gittin' any better or ther wouldn' be so many "classical" schools fer girls springin' up ever'where.

Al Moots got up as usual one mornin' an' et a hearty breakfast an' told his wife he wuz goin' t' look around fer a new hat, an' exactly thirty minutes after tryin' on a hat an' lookin' in th' triple mirrors an' seein' th' back of his neck, his body wuz found behind th' livery stable with a bullet-hole in his temple.

Mrs. Lester Meadows, who is visitin' in Morgantown, will go under th' knife from there.

Th' full-pane, clear-vision letter envelopes are purty nifty, an' we know nothin' awful has happened, that some one hain't died, when we receive one.

"I'd go t' Detroit an' drive my new car home if I thought I could control my appetite," says Pony Mopps.

Photergraphs cabled from London look like they must have lots o' eczemy over there.

NAMIN' CHILDREN

Mrs. Leghorn Tharp

Ther's been quite a lot written in regard t' th' namin' o' children, an' a lot more should be written considerin' th' seriousness o' the subject. Too many children are sent out int' th' world with names out o' all proportion t' ther looks an' ther abilities an' ther physiques—boys an' girls who must battle ther way t' success. It's no easy thing fer a youth t' git t' th' front with a purty name an' curly hair, an' it's doubly hard if his name is Dewey. Boys shouldn' be named till ther fifteen. That's th' time t' size 'em up an' name 'em Dan or Albert, or Kenneth or Stanley, or Godfrey or Cecil, or Steve or Norman, but beware o' th' name Bolivar. Never name a boy after a successful father t' grow up an' fail, an' what's still worse, never name a son after a worthless dad t' grow up an' try t'

A Rude Disappointment

keep his identity under cover. Never name a scrawny, thin spaced son Robert jest because he has a rich uncle named Robert,

87

fer money he gits that way won't do him no good. Don't give a son a double name t' split up an' rearrange an' fool with all through life. A boy with an illustrious name won't git very fer unless he's endowed. He should not try t' start even with a great name. Jest think o' th' Lincolns an' Sumners, Grants an' Grovers we run into, practically all failures, luggin' about the names of illustrious idols, an' often goin' without food an' sleepin' in th' open. I used t' know a fairly successful feller named Felix Grubbs Craw. He wuz handicapped at both ends of his name an' in th' middle. His uncle had left him a little money t' tide over his first name, an' his mother had deeded him the family home t' help out his last name. He wuz a good, industrious feller an' got on fairly well, although his middle name made it very difficult. I often wonder what would have become o' him if he'd been turned adrift without funds. Never name a boy Al unless you want ever'buddy in town t' be runnin' t' him fer favors. An' another name that's allus taken advantage of is Jack. Th' girls love it, an' that's why so few Jacks are ever heard of after they reach thirty. Women seem t' git on fairly well with incongruous names, but nothin' kin hold a woman back if she's got a sweet disposition. It's a mistake, o' course, t' name a girl Goldie, fer so many o' them fail t' return when they go t' th' grocery.

Mother kin flare up, or burn a roast, or tell th' family where t' head in, but thank goodness she hain't got two or three other jobs waitin' fer her any time she wants t' quit.

A fairly good-lookin', designin' woman has got any man beat a mile when it comes t' hypnotic power an' cruel cunnin', an' that's why we never see any male snake charmers.

Hain't it funny how quick we regain our senses after we git away from a salesman?

Talk about hard luck. Mrs. Ike Lark has got an exclusive piece o' gossip, but nobuddy t' stay with her children while she puts it out.

Henry Ford hain't only allus been a very busy man, but he's kept all th' rest o' th' country on th' jump.

Th' ole-time statesmen used t' vote as they shot, but t'day's statesmen git half-shot an' then vote, or git shot, I don't know jest how t' put it, but I've seen 'em lit up jest after they'd voted dry.

They still have English sparrows in Chicago.

One o' th' oldest an' meanest tricks in th' business is droppin' your girl till after Christmus, but it's still quite pop'lar.

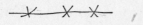

Tell Binkley has had his mustache dyed a beautiful Fascisti black.

Figures don't lie, but there's a lot o' them on th' streets that look a little too open an' above board.

Out o' all th' hundreds o' thousan's o' folks playin' golf only a pitiable per cent o' them ever' git t' be better'n fourth raters, an' it's th' same in all our callin's an' professions an' businesses. Even when it comes t' shovelin', we're woefully lackin' in fancy shovelers.

"Git away from me. You've got my knees full o' runners now," said Mrs. Lafe Bud t' her baby, who's jest beginnin' t' walk.

Ther's at least one instance where havin' enough rope didn' end disastrously, an' that's Will Rogers.

Any kind of a farm bill would be a great relief t' th' public.

Another good thing t' paste in your hat is that we're only ole once.

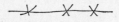

Women are certainly forgin' ahead an' identifyin' 'emselves with all th' great social an' p'litical activities of our national life, an' I wouldn' be surprised if th' time 'll come when what they have t' say 'll be taken seriously.

Life's jest one new dandruff cure after another.

No matter what's she's doin', how she's dressed, or even if she's in a bathtub, a woman should beat it th' moment she sees her estranged husband comin' up th' walk.

"Ther hain't nothin' better'n a pair o' book ends t' knock a husban' off," declares Mrs. Em Moots.

Nothin' seems t' stop dandruff as effectively as a blue serge coat.

94

Ther seem t' be more wide, invitin' an' well-paved routes t' th' cemetery than any place else.

I'm allus hearin' somebuddy say, "Well, women are certainly comin' into ther own," when they've long since left ther own an' busted into ours.

My idee o' self-confidence is walkin' right in an' buyin' a straw hat without havin' a friend along.

I kin recall when th' only time th' expression, "right o' way," wuz used when a railroad wanted t' run through a cemetery.

95

INDOOR ETIQUETTE

BY

MISS FAWN LIPPINCUT

Now that we've bid good-by t' garden parties, mountain climbin', an' such, an' plunged headlong int' th' winter's social season, a word or two about indoor social etiquette won't be amiss.

Money borrowed from a host or hostess, without security, t' tide o'er an evenin' should be returned before 10 A. M., th' next mornin'.

It reflects neglected breedin' t' tell how much your dinner suit set you back.

Never quote or refer t' prominent people like you drilled with 'em.

Don't say much o' anything is th' best rule.

Never urge a gentleman or lady t' drink.

His or her stomach may be off, which is ther inalienable right.

Never Do Any Urgin'

Where all but one of a party git a start at th' same time, it is not proper t' urge drinks too fast on th' belated guest.

In bribin' an orchestry leader never display more than enough money t' answer th' purpose.

Never tell how your wife cooks this or that.

In closeup, or Chicago, dancin' allus look around before backin' from one room t' another.

A born gentleman clears his throat on th' verandy or in th' yard.

No thoroughbred gentleman or lady 'll ask a host or hostess where they got it. If you are skeptical, which is your right, wait thirty or forty minutes after you've seen some other guest drink from th' same shaker.

All married couples should wait until they're safely within ther own boudoir before settlin' ther differences. A true lady or gentleman remains at home with a grouch same as if they had pneumonia.

In standin' up when a lady joins you don't try t' stamp your trousers down.

A perfect gentleman 'll never lengthen or shorten a suspender in polite society.

I don't know how Californy climate affects folks in general, but murderers who chop little children up seem t' live a long while out there.

Th' average married woman has so much leisure that ther hain't much else fer her t' do but repent, unless she likes t' gossip or t' play cards.

Kiss an' make up, humph! Kiss an' wash up sounds more like it.

99

A light vote allus means a lot o' light-weight office-holders.

In th' years t' come when one of our present-day youngsters has th' presidency almost within his grasp, it's goin' t' be purty tough t' have some one bob up an' say, "I kin remember when he'd steal th' first car he came to."

If you don't think th' world's purty small after all, jest you buy a dollar down set o' O. Henry, an' then try t' hide.

Talk about crawlin' out of a wrecked coupe. I'll bet a family fight in a dinette is a mess.

Surely ours is th' land o' th' brave, fer Windsor Kale walked fer nearly three blocks after dark with seven dollars in his pocket.

Bootlegger Ike Lark still quotes th' same ole prices—six dollars a quart when he hain't bein' molested, an' twelve after he's jest been raided.

Th' fine thing about spell-bindin' on th' air is that ther's no committees at th' depot t' meet you, an' you don't have t' git your neck shaved an' change your shirt.

101

It's about time nature wuz profitin' by a few of her mistakes, fer rhubarb nearly allus follers too close on th' heels of a tough winter.

Faint heart never won fair lady, or got past th' front door tryin' t' sell a vacuum sweeper.

Young squirts that speed around town till two or three o'clock in th' mornin' had better save ther roadsters fer th' long, dull, terrible evenin's an' Sundays after they're married.

Women's tiny wrist-watches come in mighty handy if you want t' know what time it used t' be.

Daylight savin' only means that mother has t' put th' coffee-pot on an hour earlier, an' hold supper till it got too dark t' see th' ball.

"Yes, Mamie's still in college, but several burlesque shows have been after her," says Mrs. Em Moots.

Who recalls when a pound o' strong butter used t' wreck th' home ever so often?

BOOTLEGGIN'

BY

IKE LARK

"TH' TIME has come t' dignify bootleggin', t' apply all th' methods an' ethics an' practises that have built up all other American business enterprises until they've become th' envy of all th' world. We kin all recall th' ole slipshod open saloon, with its heavy overhead, baseball scores, free bologna, cold slaw, rye bread an' soup, music, an' th' heavy toll it paid t' policemen an' th' bosses o' both p'litical parties. If bootleggin' is t' endure an' protect itself it must organize. We must set our house in order, an' strive t' put our business on a lofty plane. We must profit by th' mistakes o' th' licensed saloon with its pitfalls an' questionable oil paintin's.

We must safeguard our standin' with society. We are young, yit no industry 'cept th' aluminum business, has ever made

Ike Lark Speakin'

such rapid growth, an' it's fostered. I have some very pronounced ideas about bootleggin'. I have my own ideas about truckin' an' labelin', and telephonin', th' handlin' o' downtown office buldin's an' th' private home, an' dark corner deliveries. We have many complaints from some of our best an' most influential people, public officials an' folks prominent in many ways. Important plans have been upset, hostesses embarrassed, parties an' receptions delayed, an' even weddin's postponed, on account o' tardy deliveries. Ther's been instances o' homes bein' ruined an' lives snuffed out on account o' cunnin' an' irresponsible persons bein' allowed t' engage in th' traffic. Complaints o' overchargin' reach us now an' then, an' breakage has caused a lot o' dissatisfaction. Only through close an' careful organization can these evils be corrected. Zonin', too, is desirable, as overlappin' is costly. Fines are eatin' in on th' business at an alarmin' rate thro' th' clumsiness of overzealous salesmen. Standardized quarts an' pints are desirable, as is also a fixed price fer both red an' white goods. I favor th' brief-case over all other conveyances, an' I take this occasion t' protest agin' th' overloaded overcoat. Bottle rattlin' excites suspicion. All bottles should be wrapped in heavy felt paper. I'd like t' see th' traffic in th' hands o' good sober, fresh salesmen who've never been in jail. Liquor transports should be inspected daily fer carburetor an' tire trouble. Spark plugs should be clean an' ever ready t' function. Th' habit o' drinkin' with customers jest as a guarantee o' good faith should stop. It's an unbusinesslike procedure, an' often kills or makes a drunkard of a useful salesman."

If it's dangerous t' talk t' a motorman who's movin' along on his own right o' way, how many thousan' times more hazardous is it t' nag a driver?

"I promise t' do ever'thing that's humanly possible t' bring curves back," declared Lisle Tharp, Republican cannydate fer assessor, in a speech, after sayin' that our tardy prosperity wuz caused by underconsumption o' food, an' th' fad t' be spindly.

"Ther used t' be very few avenues open t' homely people before th' art o' lookin' nifty took th' country," said Tell Binkley, as he passed Miss Myrt Purviance, who's engaged t' our leadin' banker.

108

Anyhow th' feller that incloses a few stamps fer a dandruff cure hain't out very much an' it'll be a valuable lesson fer him.

Talk about swift an' sure justice, Mrs. Ike Lark's brother, who shot a deputy sheriff Monday evenin', was tried an' in prison before daylight, as th' farm he wuz livin' on wuzn' his'n.

"Are you real sure th' sun won't fade 'em?" asked a flapper at th' Emporium, while pickin' out some bloomers.

Don't let th' politicians kid you, Mr. Farmer. Th' only friend you kin depend on is th' quail.

You kin fool most any actor with promises, but a trained seal takes no chances.

It's gittin' so th' politicians depend a lot more on those who'er too lazy t' vote than they do on those who vote.

"Well, I'm out o' luck that's all," declares Hon. Ex-Editur Cale Fluhart, who's keenly disappointed in not gittin' on th' D. A. R. blacklist.

Tilford Moots' nephew, a veteran o' Château-Thierry an' a Chicago primary, dropped in on him this fall.

110

"I'm glad my daughter had a college career fer me t' look back on, fer it wuz th' happiest an' most restful period o' my life," says Mrs. Lib Pash.

Love at first sight often turns out purty good, unless she wuz climbin' in a rumble seat.

Another Indianny bank wuz looted yisterday, this time by bandits.

I notice several of our farmers speak o' tryin' it agin next year.

111

"Oh, she'd have been rid o' him long ago, but he's got insomina an' she can't ketch him asleep," I heard a woman say.

I'd like t' attend one o' them Republican blowouts at Chicago if ther wuz any way t' tell which politician's home wuz goin' t' be blown.

"It's wonderful how some fellers ever git so rich when ther so easy t' tap," says Tell Binkley, who has allus maintained that Hardin' could have been elected fer nine or ten dollars.

Nobuddy kin talk as soft an' gentle as a dentist with his back turned huntin' among his drills fer th' most ferocious one he kin find.

Mrs. Ike Lark's married daughter, o' Oklahomy, who's visitin' her, cries nearly all the time. She imagines her husband is gittin' so rich he'll kick her out.

Wilbur Pine got drunk t'day t' keep from bein' called a fanatic.

Th' father who tries t' make a pal of his son these days will have to go some.

113

BANKRUPT MARRIAGE CROP, ETC.

BY

LESTER KITE

TH' BANKRUPT marriage crop has reached proportions that endangers th' very life o' th' republic, clogs th' courts, an' demoralizes th' installment business. Marriages do not hit th' junk heap with suddenness. Sometimes th' collapse starts long before th' weddin'. Carefully gathered statistics show that fellers who marry at thirty or thirty-five, or after they've saved a hundred dollars or so, hold out th' longest, an' that women who give up at thirty an' marry are more liable t' make th' best o' things an' stay put. Split-ups come on gradually, an' may start from th' most trivial matters, such as hunger, lack o' shoes, absence o' diversion, or tryin' t' eat

breakfast together. Too much money,
however, causes more marital failures
than poverty. Most women love freedom

No Surprise

an' in these latter days they're showin' a
cravin' fer thrills that hain't doin' th'
home any good. In th' ole days th' saloon

had much t' do with many domestic wrecks, but t'day when th' husband an' wife both drink, th' smash up is retarded fer a year or two. Sometimes in th' last few years there seems t' be a tendency among mothers an' fathers t' divide th' assets an' split up after th' children are married—a sort o' beginnin' over movement. This fad is th' outgrowth o' club life, an' th' determination on th' part o' so many t' carry on long after they're due t' settle down an' stay at home. So many of us don't seem t' be satisfied with anything these days. We're restless an' amusement mad, an' it's little wonder that anything as sacred as marriage, or as gentle an' restful as a home, fails t' appeal t' married folks. So many parents, those who stay married, expect th' public schools t' train an' discipline ther children when ther small, an' colleges an' private schools t' watch over them thro' th' critical periods o' ther lives. An'

116

here's another thought—parents have jest about reached th' point where they hain't got th' time an' patience t' fool with children. Th' desire t' live twice on th' same earth is th' blightin' fad o' th' present era.

Our unemployment parade yisterday wuz a big success, some three hundred an' thirty-three cars bein' in th' procession.

Elmer Small fell off a load o' hay an' died before he could have his teeth X-rayed.

117

"When I wuz a boy I'd jump at th' chance t' wash a phaeton jest fer permission t' use it awhile Sunday afternoon," said Judge Pusey, while three or four mothers wuz pleadin' fer ther sons.

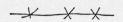

Our commercial club turned down a big convention at ther' meetin' t'-day 'cause prohibition officials allus try t' make a town dry when ther's anything goin' on.

"Out o' one hundred an' nineteen cases o' husban' slippin' that come before me in 1928, one hundred an' eighteen wuz traced directly t' th' husban' havin' t' pile out in all sorts o' weather an' git his breakfast downtown," declares Judge Pusey.

I don't know which gits discouraged first—th' girl who marries fer a home, or th' feller who expects t' git rich raisin' squabs fer th' market, but it must be a purty close race.

"Oh, if I only had a car I'd try on some hats," said Miss Fawn Lippincut, as she passed an empty parkin' space directly in front o' th' Elite Millinery Emporium.

They probe th' bosses instead of th' elections in Chicago.

It's a lucky wife that don't fade before her husband gits rich.

"Is our taste fer th' legitimate theater dyin' out? Is ther no longer a dependable clientele fer th' spoken drammer? Has our vaunted love fer th' artistic waned? No, folks jest won't pay five an' six dollars," says Tell Binkley.

Bank robbers seem t' git off twice as easy as fellers who marry fer money.

It's goin' some t' live once these days, hereafter or no hereafter.

"Oh, I seem t' be in th' way, an' I sometimes feel that those about me would be fer better off if I tried t' cross th' street," says Gran'maw Pash.

It's a wonder honesty don't pay better considerin' all th' competition it's up against.

Next t' an invitational affair nothin' leaves as many sore spots as fallin' off a stepladder with an arm full o' window curtains.

Somethin' else that's becomin' rarer ever'day is home-grown daughters.

Some fellers are elected hands down, but most o' them have ther hands tied.

Mrs. Tilford Moots' niece writes that she went t' hear Will Rogers an' he "waxed" eloquent.

It hain't been so long since th' whole country wuz excited over th' lost Charley Ross, an' t'day no home's complete without a missin' daughter.

Artie Mapes an' his wife split up yisterday after havin' only been married two months. He allowed her seventy-two sherbet glasses, an' he took th' seven electric toasters.

Judge Pusey is slowly recoverin' from th' evidence offered in th' Bootlegger Ike Lark case.

ATHLETICS AN' DOCTORIN'

Mrs. Lide Hanger

Mrs. Tipton Bud received a pustal-card this week from her nephew out in Kansas sayin' that his wife has lately had a liver attack an' it took fourteen hours t' find a doctor. He says his town has five doctors, all contendin' fer a golf trophy but one, an' he's th' president o' th' gun club an' secretary o' th' Sunflower Chess Association. But Kansas doctors hain't no different from doctors ever'where. Lafe Bud doubled up an' toppled over th' other day, an' it wuz a week before his wife could run down Doctor Mopps. "Where have you got him?" Doc asked her. "He's in bed at home," she said. "Well, git his

123

teeth X-rayed an' haul him t' th' hospital an' I'll be around t'-morrow an' look him over," said Doc, as he entered a sportin' goods store. Well about ten o'clock th' next day Doc went t' th' hospital an' looked Lafe over, an' said, "Well, I'll have t' cut him open. Jest starve him fer two or three days an' call me at th' country club an' I'll see what I kin do fer him." It takes almost as long t' find a doctor an' git him in th' notion o' tacklin' a case as it does t' git an adjustment at a laundry. Th' family doctor o' th' past is fast passin' away. He wuzn' so handy with tools as th' modern doctor, but he wuz allus on th' job rain or shine, or on circus day. He wuz trusted an' revered. If a feller wuz goin' t' trade a horse or build a new house, or embark on an adventure o' any sort, he'd first consult his family doctor. Sometimes th' family doctor would be called in th' middle o' th' night t' help out on th' plans fer a new stable, or talk some wife out o' th' notion o' gittin' a divorce. When th' ole family doctor used t' die he left a stack of ac-

Dr. Mopps

counts behind as high as a jail window, but when th' modern doctor passes on he leaves a pile o' golf clubs. If Doc Mopps wuz t' die on th' links t'day he'd leave a comfortable fortune tied up in golf stockin's alone. An appendix operation only means another dozen pair o' imported golf stockin's t' him. It seems t' me ther's an awful good openin' in any town fer a good steady doctor that don't care fer athletics.

Lots o' folks would like t' know what "fascism" is, but they don't know how t' pronounce what it is they want t' ask about.

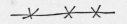

Th' Colonial Bridge Club met t'day t' knock Wesley Moots' new wife.

126

No matter how much strong black coffee we drink, most any after-dinner speech 'll counteract it.

Our Ladies Aid Society reports that it recently found three families completely out o' gas, an' one wretched hovel where th' family had been unable t' git about fer three days owin' t' a blowout.

With father payin' ten times as much fer liquor as formerly, an' th' appallin' cost o' keepin' mother beautiful, it's a lucky youngster that even gits an orange this Christmus.

I'll bet a Spitzbergen night club is a nice sleepy affair.

It wuz thought fer awhile this mornin' that Joe Lark had dropped dead in front o' th' Emporium, but he wuz layin' on his back tryin t' read th' price tag on a loungin' robe.

Who recalls th' good ole days when ther wuz a long closed season fer carrots?

I never like t' ask where th' mail-box is in a hotel 'cause I'm allus standin' right by it.

128

"O' course we wuz tickled t' death t' see her, but she makes so much ashes," said Mrs. Finley Mopps, whose daughter is home from school fer th' holidays.

Th' sympathy o' th' entire community goes out t' Mr. Lemmie Peters who caught a sailfish at Miammy an' didn' have money enough t' git it mounted.

I expect lots o' th' married men who tiptoe out in th' mornin' an' close th' door softly an' git an egg downtown would rather fight after th' busy worries o' th' day.

129

Next t' a dolphin ther hain't nothin' that droops an' fades like a lady-killer after he's hooked.

"Oh, boy, but it feels good t' git in a reg'lar bed after layin' on a hard floor," says Cashier Al Mopps, o' th' Skunk Ridge Bank.

"If I had my way about it a feller with mackerel eyes, a cow-lick, an' shirt open at th' neck, couldn' git a license t' marry," declares Constable Plum, in explainin' how easy it is t' detect a potential wife murderer.

Th' worst waste o' breath, next t' play-in' a saxophone, is advisin' a son.

I hain't seen that purty girl in th' car-pet-sweeper ads fer a long time, an' I do wonder if she's gone an' made a fool of herself.

Little Myrtle Pash wuz awarded th' general knowledge cup at Skunk Ridge School this fall fer namin' th' junior sen-ator o' Idaho.

Remember when corn cure ads only showed th' foot?

Mrs. Pogue Swallow's nephew, out in Californy, has confessed t' murderin' his mother in Indianny jest t' git back t' good ole Indianny.

Th' feller that puts off marryin' till he kin support a wife hain't very much in love.

Remember when we used to look up t' women?

Another good way t' tell a railroad crossin', if you can't read, is by th' hump in th' road.

MORE ON PHYSIOGNOMY

BY

MRS. POGUE SWALLOW

PROFESSOR Hawk, physiognomist, room 8, New Palace Hotel, is closin' his last an' most successful week. Many have called t' have ther heads looked over, all seemin' anxious t' git started in th' right avenues t' success before it's too late. As a result ther's considerable shiftin' about in our professional an' commercial life. Joe Pine has resigned as president o' th' Skunk Ridge Bank an' 'll take advantage o' th' fullness over his ears an' become a rear admiral. Art Lark stopped auto paintin' over night t' become an expert advertisin' man. Pictures an' findin's o' class No. 2 accompany this article, an' may be read with profit.

No. 1.   Lisle Spar, saxophone, Purdue, '23. Note th' long stretch from th' point o' th' chin t' th' ear an' across up t' th' eye denotin' lack o' rhythm an' harmony, an' an almost ravenous aptness fer successful celery raisin', or as th' guidin' genius o' some gigantic colonization project. Th' caved in condition about th' mouth indicates a fondness fer solitaire an' a pronounced aversion fer details. Mr. Spar is still a young man an' 'll doubtless make a change if he kin sell his cow.

No. 2.   Mrs. Leghorn Tharp. Note th' square, well-set head, an' fierce, commandin' jaws, liberal eyebrows, an' eagle nose. This subject is a born leader in any atmosphere she finds herself in. She has all th' bumps of an organizer an' leader, but she didn' know it when she married th' driver of a dressed poultry delivery wagon. T'day she's held back by a family

o' eight an' a furnace, all because she didn'
git her head examined.

No. 3. Tell Binkley, tornado insur-

Telltale Faces

ance agent. Th' average layman lookin' at
this picture would pronounce th' subject
a man o' big affairs, a forceful man, a steel

trust director, an' a man o' vision. Th'
keen physiognomist is not so easily taken
in, however. Note th' full elevated eyebrows, th' bulbous nose, lodge jewelry, an'
close-reefed wire mustache, th' smug expression o' th' eyes, an' note how th' ears
stick close t' th' skull, all o' which are un-
mistakable indications of a four-flusher.

No. 4. Ike Lark, bootlegger. Note th'
unusually healthy mustache on this subject, th' small twinklin' eyes, fine nose, an'
standard forehead. Note that th' ears have
no lobes. Ther's none o' th' telltale marks
o' th' criminal, or evil doer, about this subject. He'd pass anywhere as a small merchant, or an authority on bees, or a lover
o' flowers. If he had had his head examined in early manhood we doubtless
would have heard of him as a ventril-
oquist. Or he could have been an inter-
nationally famous peony grower.

Women are th' limit. A Newcastle, Pennsylvania, woman has gone t' Valparaiso, Indianny, t' spend th' summer with her husban's first wife, while he lays out a sentence at Youngstown, Ohio.

We all make mistakes, but ther's no excuse fer anybuddy havin' a full-front photograph taken, even if they have been nominated fer somethin'.

I used t' think if I wuz rich I'd buy a barber's chair t' lay in, but now I believe I'd buy a big, solid iron automobile.

137

While Lisle Tharp wuz tryin' t' thumb his way t' Bloom Center, Butcher Joe Mopps drove along, an' takin' a fancy t' his thumb, he hired him t' clerk in his meat-shop.

Th' complete new cottage o' Mr. an' Mrs. Ainsley Putnam is nearin' completion, an'll have five bathrooms, two bars, an' other modern conveniences.

Ever'thing else has about reached th' limit, but so fer none o' th' big cigarette posters shows a beautiful girl smokin' one o' th' things.

138

It's goin' t' be fun t' watch an' see how long th' meek kin keep the earth after they inherit it.

You never kin tell what a country jury, or a delegate that washes down a hot dog sandwich with strawberry pop, is goin' t' do.

While ever'buddy appears t' be gittin' along, times 'll never be what lots o' folks would call ideal till we have easy payment fillin' stations.

An optimist is a feller that digs dandelions out o' his lawn.

Lester Lark, o' th' Weekly Sliphorn, won th' Tell Binkley prize fer th' best write-up of a burnin' buildin', bein' th' only contestant that didn' say anything about th' flames "belchin' forth" an' th' structure bein' "gutted."

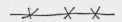

No matter how much money a woman's got she can't dress up-to-date unless she's also got th' nerve.